Helping Children See Jesus

ISBN: 978-1-64104-034-1

Jehovah
Old Testament Volume 30: Psalms

Author: Ruth B. Greiner
Illustrator: Vernon Henkel
Computer Graphic Artists: Olivia and Bethany Moy
Typesetting and Layout: Patricia Pope

© 2019 Bible Visuals International
PO Box 153, Akron, PA 17501-0153
Phone: (717) 859-1131
www.biblevisuals.org

All rights reserved. No part of this publication may be reproduced, stored in a retrieval system or transmitted in any form by any means, electronic, mechanical, photocopy, recording or otherwise, without the prior permission of the publisher, except as provided by USA copyright law.

RELATED ITEMS

To access related items (such as activities, memory verse posters and translated texts) please visit our web store at www.biblevisuals.org and enter 2030 at the top right of the web page. You may need to reduce the zoom setting to get the search box.

FREE TEXT DOWNLOAD

To obtain a FREE printable copy of the English teaching text (PDF format) under Product Format, please scroll down and select Extra–PDF Teacher Text Download. Then under Language select English before clicking the ADD TO CART button to place in your shopping cart. Other languages are available at an additional cost from the Language menu. When checking out, use coupon code XTACSV17 at checkout and click on Apply Coupon to receive the discount on the English text.

NAMES OF GOD:
JEHOVAH
JEHOVAH-jireh
JEHOVAH-shalom
ELOHIM

The **LORD** knoweth the way of the righteous: but the way of the ungodly shall perish. Psalm 1:6

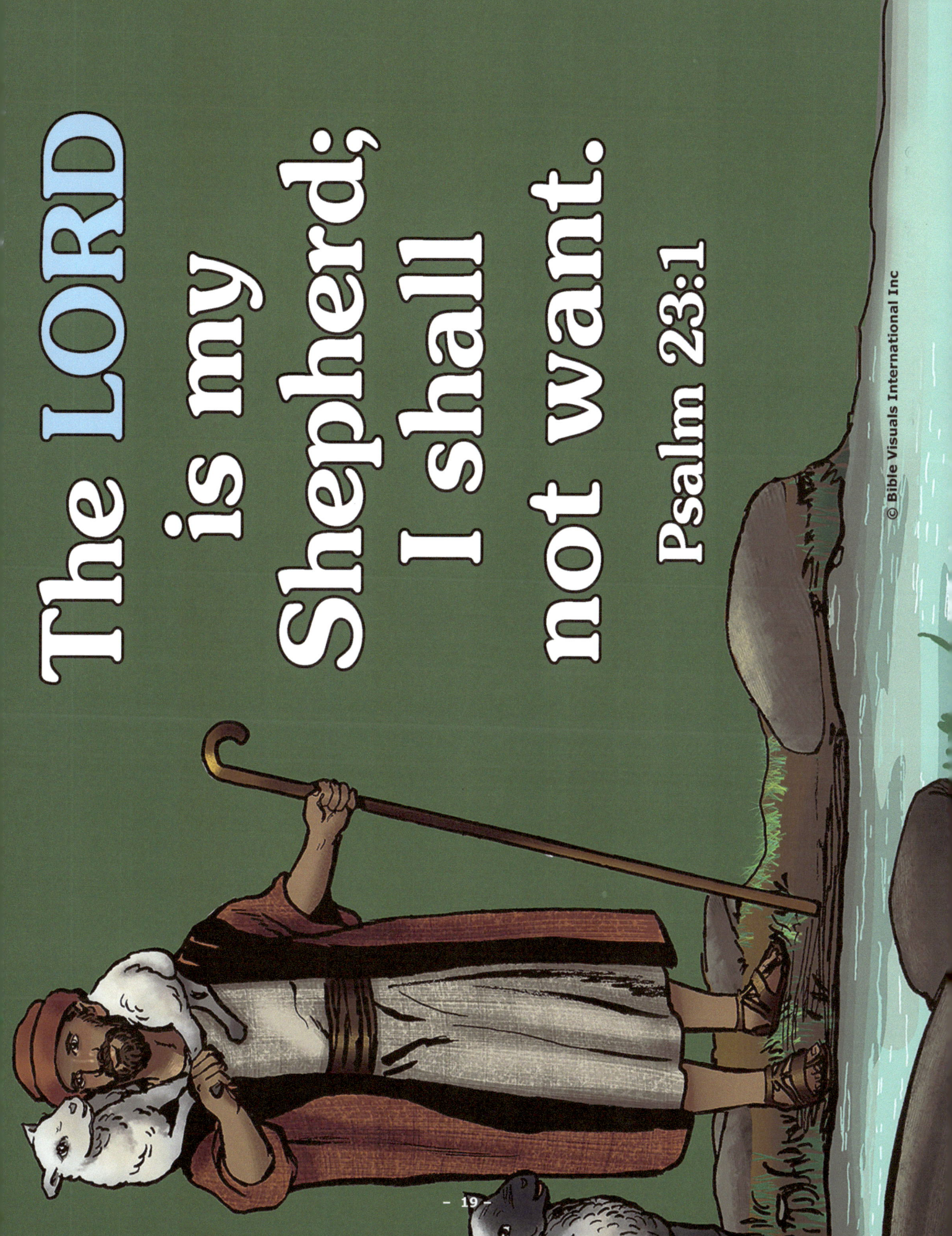

The LORD will bless His people with peace.

Psalm 29:11b

I will praise Thee, O LORD, with my whole heart; I will shew forth all Thy marvelous works. Psalm 9:1

Lesson 1
JEHOVAH'S WAYS

> **NOTE TO THE TEACHER**
>
> In this series we shall study only a few of the 150 psalms. There are many kinds of psalms: psalms of praise, prayer psalms, prophetic psalms, and others. Prophetic psalms tell of Jesus Christ, hundreds of years before His birth.
>
> Each of these lessons includes a wonderful name for the LORD. These names are from the Hebrew, the original language of the Old Testament. Print each name on a separate poster. On reverse side of poster, print the meaning of the name. Review every name in each lesson.
>
> For this first lesson, on one side of poster print in all capital letters: LORD GOD=JEHOVAH
>
> On reverse side of poster, print the following meanings of JEHOVAH's name. (The Scripture references are for your study, Teacher. Do not include them on poster.)
>
> He is holy (Exodus 15:11; Leviticus 11:44-45). So . . . He hates sin and must punish it (Genesis 3:13-19). But . . . He loves the sinner (Genesis 3:21; Isaiah 53:6).
>
> There are additional meanings for the name JEHOVAH. For simplicity, we suggest teaching only these at this time.
>
> In the English King James version of the Bible, the name JEHOVAH appears by itself only in Exodus 6:3; Psalm 83:18; Isaiah 12:2; 26:4.
>
> In many versions, watch for GOD or LORD in all capital letters. (See for example, Genesis 6:5-8; 15:2,8.) GOD or LORD means JEHOVAH [YAHWEH]. Whenever the name GOD or LORD or JEHOVAH appears in the Bible, He is reminding us of His holiness. It is such a holy name that in early times it was not spoken aloud.
>
> Are you teaching a language other than English? If so, check your Bible carefully to see the LORD GOD's names.

Scriptures to be studied: Psalms 1:1-6; 8:1-9; 18:1-32; 25:1-12

The *aim* of the lesson: To show the importance of choosing JEHOVAH's way.

   What your students should *know*: JEHOVAH, the holy One, loves us but hates our sinful way.

   What your students should *feel*: A desire to please JEHOVAH.

   What your students should *do*: Choose now to walk in JEHOVAH's way.

Lesson outline (for the teacher's and students' notebooks):

1. People choose their way (Psalm 1:1-6).
2. JEHOVAH's surprising way (Psalm 8:1-9).
3. JEHOVAH's perfect way (Psalm 18:1-32).
4. JEHOVAH teaches His way (Psalm 25:1-12).

The verse to be memorized:

The LORD knoweth the way of the righteous: but the way of the ungodly shall perish. (Psalm 1:6)

Teacher: Depending upon the age of your students, encourage them to memorize the entire psalm.

THE LESSON

How many names do you have? Two? Three? Does anyone have 20 names? Listen to this: The LORD GOD of Heaven has even more than 20 names! Each of His names has a special meaning. One of His names is God. (That is Elohim.) In the first verse of the Bible we read: "In the beginning God . . ." This is the name Elohim. (Have students look at Genesis 1:1.) When God is written this way, it means He is the strong One. He is so strong that He spoke, and everything everywhere was created! So when we read *God* in the Bible, we think of His great strength.

In English Bibles, GOD and LORD are sometimes printed in all capital letters. Either GOD or LORD (all capitals) mean JEHOVAH. He uses this wonderful name for Himself to let us know He loves us. (*Teacher:* Show poster.) The LORD GOD, JEHOVAH, is holy. Because He is holy, He hates my sin and must punish it. But He loves me. Together let us say reverently:

JEHOVAH is holy. He hates my sin and must punish it. But He loves me. Remember this when you read LORD or GOD or JEHOVAH in the Bible.

Near the center of the Bible is its longest book–Psalms. Psalms are songs. The shepherd David (who became king of Israel), wrote about half the psalms. There are short psalms and long psalms. God's special name LORD (meaning JEHOVAH) is used in all but 18 of the psalms. (*Teacher:* Give your students opportunity to look for LORD in the psalms. Point out the difference between LORD [all capitals] and Lord [capital L only]. If your students do not understand the difference between capital and small letters, do not teach the meaning of Lord at this time.)

When Lord (capital L only–print on blackboard) is used, it means He is Master. LORD (all capitals) means He is holy, loving, and hates sin. We should read the Bible carefully, remembering even the meanings of God's names.

1. PEOPLE CHOOSE THEIR WAY
Psalm 1:1-6

We do not know who wrote the first psalm. But this we know about him: he was a holy (*set apart by God*) man. Through him, God's Holy Spirit spoke. (See 2 Timothy 3:16; 2 Peter 1:21.) Let us imagine that the writer of the first psalm is here with us today. Open your Bible to the first psalm and listen to the psalmist.

Show Illustration #1

"There are two kinds of people in the world going two different ways. (1) There are godly people. They love God and have chosen to walk in His way. (Point to narrow way on left.) (2) There are ungodly people. They love themselves and want to go their own way. Let me tell you first about godly people." (Have students look at Psalm 1:1.)

"*Blessed* (very, very happy) is the person who chooses God's way. This godly person does not behave like ungodly people (see verse 1). The godly person does not: (1) *Walk* (go around) with ungodly people; (2) Ask ungodly people for advice on what to do (*counsel*); (3) *Stand* around, doing the same as the ungodly; (4) *sit down* with those who make fun of God.

"Do you understand?" (*Teacher:* encourage questions.)

Now see how the godly person does behave. "The godly person loves to read God's Word, the Bible. It is *the law of the LORD* (*JEHOVAH*). (See verse 2.) JEHOVAH's law tells of His holiness. It tells that He hates sins. It speaks of JEHOVAH's love for sinners–and much, much more. Do you read His Word every *day*? Do you *meditate*, think about what it says, even at *night*?" (Let students discuss.)

"The godly person is *like a tree planted by rivers of water* (verse 3). (Point to tree and water.) This means the godly person is strong for the LORD and *prospers*. (He receives good from the LORD.) The LORD (JEHOVAH) *watches over the way of the righteous* (godly) person (verse 6). The godly person chooses God's way which leads to Heaven. (Point to rays at top left of Illustration #1.) No wonder the person who goes God's way is very happy!

"It is much different for ungodly people who choose their own way. They choose to do wrong instead of obeying God. These wrong-doers are worthless, *like chaff* (the outside shell of rice or wheat) *which the wind blows away*. (Read Psalm 1:4-6.) *The way of the ungodly shall perish.* The ungodly go away from the LORD who loves them. Their way leads to a dreadful place of awful fire and darkness. (Point to lower right of Illustration #1.) There they will be punished and separated from God forever."

Let us say our verse together. (Have students read or quote Psalm 1:6.)

Are you going your own ungodly way? If so, please talk to me after class.

2. JEHOVAH'S SURPRISING WAY
Psalm 8:1-9

The shepherd David, who wrote many psalms, usually lived according to JEHOVAH's way. He carefully tended his sheep day and night. He had lots of time to look at the wonderful world God had created. He studied the beautiful flowers and trees. He watched the birds in the sky and fish in the waters. David, knowing everything had been made by God, wanted to thank Him. David played the harp well. (See 1 Samuel 16:14-23.) So with his harp and with singing he praised JEHOVAH.

One of his songs (Psalm 8) begins: "O LORD (*JEHOVAH*) our Lord (*Master*)." David praised JEHOVAH, the holy One who hates sin and punishes it. (Display poster.) David added, "Your name, LORD, is excellent in all the earth!" (Psalm 8:1). David loved the LORD and loved to sing His name.

Show Front Cover

Looking at the sky at night, David continued his praise song to JEHOVAH: He sang "You have set Your glory above the heavens" (verse 1b). David understood that the glorious LORD lives above the beautiful heavens. He sang, "The heavens, the moon, the stars, are the work of Your fingers, O LORD" (verse 3).

David would have seen Orion, Pleiades, the Big Dipper always in place in the heavens. (*Teacher:* Name constellations familiar to your students.) Thinking of the wonders of the starry skies, he sang, "What is man that You, Lord, think of Him?" David was surprised that the God of the huge universe thinks about mere people. Then David remembered: "You, LORD, made people to have charge over the works of Your hands." (See verses 4-6; Genesis 1:26.)

Show Illustration #2

David went on singing: "You (*JEHOVAH*) put people over sheep, oxen, goats, fowls of the air, the fish of the sea, the whole earth" (verses 7-8). God is Creator of everything. He wanted David (and He wants all of us) to take care of His marvelous creation. This is JEHOVAH's surprising way. Do you help to care for all God created–trees, flowers, animals, everything?

The shepherd David closed his psalm singing this praise: "O LORD (JEHOVAH), our Lord (Master), how excellent is Your name in all the earth!" (verse 9). We, too, can praise the LORD right now with these same words. (Have students say verse reverently.)

3. JEHOVAH'S PERFECT WAY
Psalm 18:1-32

King Saul (Israel's first king) had real problems. At times he raged wildly. One of Saul's servants knew the shepherd David was a good harpist. He said to the king, "David plays the harp. He is brave and the LORD (JEHOVAH) is with him." Immediately King Saul sent for David and, seeing him, liked him at once. He even chose David to be his armor-bearer. Then, whenever an evil spirit made the king scream wildly, David played his harp. And that would end King Saul's wild raging. (See 1 Samuel 16:14-23.)

After David killed the enemy giant, Goliath, David became a hero. This caused King Saul to be very jealous of David. Then an evil spirit came on Saul and he was like a madman. He hurled his spear at David, hoping to kill him. But David escaped. (See 1 Samuel 18:6-16; also 19:9-10.)

This was only the beginning. For a long, long time (years!) David ran, hid, and kept escaping from King Saul. There were times when David could have killed the king. But he was too honorable to do something so wicked. (See 1 Samuel 24:1-13; 26:1-23.)

Finally King Saul died on the battlefield. Afterward David, remembering his awful experiences, sang a meaningful song. (Have students turn to Psalm 18. First read the introductory statement. Observe that this song appears also in 2 Samuel 22.)

Show Illustration #3

Here is part of David's song: "I love You, O LORD (JEHOVAH), my strength. The LORD (*the holy one*) is my rock, my fortress, my rescuer; My God (*the strong One*) is my rock . . . He is my shield . . . I call to the LORD . . . and I am saved from my enemies" (verses 1-3).

David had hidden behind huge rocks and in forts where Saul did not find him. Yet David understood that he had been protected by God Himself.

There were times when David almost died (read verses 3-5). Then he cried to God and God heard him (verse 6).

So David sang, "The LORD (JEHOVAH) rescued me from my enemies who were too strong for me" (verse 17). David included this testimony in his song: "I have kept the ways of the LORD. I have not done evil by turning from my God" (verse 21). David added, "As for God, His way is perfect." And ". . . it is God who gives me strength and makes my way perfect" (verses 30-32). He helps me to go His way.

Do you honor the LORD? Can you honestly say, "I have kept the ways of the LORD and not turned from God"? Whatever happens to you, do you remember, "As for God, His way is perfect"? Do you truly believe that God makes your way perfect? (Have students tell how God protected them in times of danger.)

4. JEHOVAH TEACHES HIS WAY
Psalm 25:1-12

Have you wondered how David could know God's way? We learn the answer to this from his prayer in Psalm 25. (Have students follow in their Bibles.)

He began: "To You, O LORD (JEHOVAH), I pray. O my God, I trust in You" (verses 1-2). David continued, "Show me (*make clear to me*) Your ways, O LORD" (verse 4). We must ask the LORD to show us what we should or should not do.

Years later, the Lord told King Solomon: "Ask Me for what you want." And Solomon prayed, "O LORD my God, I am like a little child. Give me understanding so I can know right from wrong" (1 Kings 3:5-9). The great Solomon (like his father, David) asked to be shown God's ways. Solomon truly wanted to know right from wrong. Do you? Do you ask the LORD to show you His right ways?

David also prayed, "O LORD, teach me Your paths" (verse 4). An ox-driver goads (*prods* and *drives*) his oxen. (Name animals your students know.) And David is asking God to teach (*prod, goad*) him to go the right way. David knew his own ways might be wrong. He really wanted to know God's way. Do you?

Show Illustration #4

Then David prayed, "Lead me, O LORD, in Your truth" (verse 5). He was saying, "Take me by my hand, LORD (*as a father takes his child's hand*) and lead me in Your truthful way." David sang: "Who is the person who fears (*honors, loves, obeys*) the LORD? The LORD will teach that person in the way God has chosen" (verse 12).

Do you honestly fear and truly honor JEHOVAH? Will you tell Him now that you want to do whatever He wants? If you do, He will teach you the way He has chosen for you.

Let students pray silently.

Lesson 2
JEHOVAH'S PROVISION

NOTE TO THE TEACHER

Begin by reviewing the meaning of GOD's wonderful name, JEHOVAH.

In this lesson we learn another name of GOD: JEHOVAH-Jireh. It means *The LORD will provide*. The truth of this name should grip your heart. The LORD Himself will provide what we need–not everything we want. We may not always have all the food we want or the kind we want. Sometimes God disciplines us this way. We don't want to be disciplined, nor do we enjoy it. But the LORD knows we need it.

On a poster, print JEHOVAH-Jireh. On reverse side print the meaning: "The LORD will provide." (Genesis 22:13.) Observe how students love to learn these unusual names and their meanings.

The second part of this lesson includes: (1) David's prayer for forgiveness (Psalm 51); and (2) David's praise for forgiveness (Psalm 32). In both he used the words *transgression, iniquity, sin*. As you teach the meanings of these words, print each word on Illustration #6.

On 6a print TRANSGRESSION. David is turning away from God's Law (the scroll). He knew God's Law. He had knowingly, deliberately, turned against what God commanded. This is *transgression*.

On 6b print INIQUITY. The heart is filled with dark marks. David admitted he was guilty of sin. This is iniquity.

On 6c print SIN. David, contrite, is lying face down underneath a clean, shining heart, confessing his sin. He had missed the mark, falling short of what God wanted him to be (pure and honorable=clean, shining heart. Missing the mark, falling short, is *sin*.

If your students have Bibles, let them pick out these words in Psalms 51 and 32.

Is your group memorizing the entire first psalm? If not, have them learn the verse suggested with each lesson.

Scriptures to be studied: Genesis 22:1-14; Psalms 23, 32, 51

The *aim* of the lesson: To show that JEHOVAH provides for the needs of His children.

  What your students should *know*: The Christian must trust JEHOVAH for each need.

  What your students should *feel*: The desire to look to JEHOVAH for His provision.

  What your students should *do*: Ask JEHOVAH for His forgiveness, provision, protection.

Lesson outline (for the teacher's and students' notebooks):
1. JEHOVAH provides a sacrifice (Genesis 22:1-14).
2. JEHOVAH provides forgiveness (Psalm 32).
3. JEHOVAH provides what we need (Psalm 23:1-3).
4. JEHOVAH provides now and forevermore (Psalm 23:4-6).

The verse to be memorized:

The LORD is my Shepherd; I shall not want. (Psalm 23:1)

THE LESSON

The shepherd David, who later became King David, did not have a Bible. There were no Bibles then. However, God's Law was written on scrolls. (These were like long rolls of paper.) The scrolls (containing Genesis, Exodus, Leviticus, Numbers, Deuteronomy) were kept in the temple. From the scrolls, the priests read God's Law to the people. And the people taught God's Law to their children.

1. JEHOVAH PROVIDES A SACRIFICE
Genesis 22:1-14

When David was young, his father (Jesse) would have taught him this:

"Our Father Abraham lived hundreds and hundreds of years ago. One day he took his son Isaac to the mountain to worship God. Before worshiping, Abraham first had to offer a sacrifice. On their way, young Isaac said, 'My father, we have the fire and the wood. But where is the lamb that is to be sacrificed?'

"Father Abraham answered, 'My son, God Himself will provide a lamb'."

David listened as his father continued: "On the mountain, Abraham built an altar and on it arranged the wood. Then he clutched Isaac in his arms. Tenderly, lovingly, he bound Isaac and laid him on the altar.

"Fearfully Abraham lifted his knife, ready to offer his son to God. At that moment, the angel of the LORD [JEHOVAH] called from Heaven, saying 'Abraham! Abraham! Don't touch the boy! Now I know you fear God. You've been willing to give him to Me."

Show Illustration #4

"Looking up, Abraham saw a ram caught by its horns. He seized the ram and sacrificed it instead of Isaac. God Himself had provided an animal sacrifice. So Abraham called that place *JEHOVAH-Jireh*, meaning: *The LORD will provide*." (See Genesis 22:1-14. *Teacher:* Show JEHOVAH-Jireh poster.)

From the time David heard this, he loved God's special name, JEHOVAH-Jireh. When he was a shepherd, he and his sheep had many needs. When he became king, David needed wisdom, and much more, to rule God's people. But whatever his needs, David knew JEHOVAH-Jireh, the LORD will provide.

Long, long after David, JEHOVAH-Jireh provided a marvelous plan for everyone everywhere. He sent from Heaven to earth His only Son, the Lord Jesus Christ.

Show Illustration #5

(*Teacher:* Point to cross in smoke) Christ, the perfect One, died on the cross, taking the punishment for our sins. (See Isaiah 53:6; Romans 3:23; 1 Corinthians 15:3; 1 Peter 2:24.) God accepted Christ's death as payment for our sins. (See Romans 4:25; 1 Corinthians 15:4.) Then God brought Christ back to life. Now all who truly believe in Christ Jesus receive His everlasting life. (See John 5:24.) JEHOVAH-Jireh provided the perfect sacrifice for your sin–and mine.

2. JEHOVAH PROVIDES FORGIVENESS
Psalm 32

Like everyone everywhere, King David was sometimes tempted to do wrong. Being a king did not make him perfect. So a time came when David sinned. He stole another man's wife and arranged for her husband to be killed. (See 2 Samuel 11.)

David thought no one knew he had sinned. But JEHOVAH (the holy One who hates sin) knew. (See 2 Samuel 11:27.) And he sent a man, Nathan, to talk to King David. (See 2 Samuel 12:1-15.) When Nathan finished, David realized that God saw all his wickedness. Sadly David cried, "I have sinned against the LORD(JEHOVAH)."

Show Illustration #6

Turning to JEHOVAH, David prayed, "Have mercy on me, O God." (Have students follow his confession in Psalm 51.) "Blot out my *TRANSGRESSIONS*." David was saying, "I *purposely turned against Your Law, O God*." (Point to illustration #6a.) "Wash away all my *INIQUITY* (guilt). I have missed the mark, falling short of what You, God, want me to be." (Point to illustration 6b.)

David continued his confession, praying, "Against You, You only (God) I have sinned. I have done evil in Your sight. Hide your face from my sins. Blot out my many guilty acts. Create in me a clean (pure) heart, O God." (See Psalm 51:1, 2, 4, 9, 10.)

David prayed all this and more when he asked God's forgiveness. Do you think the LORD heard him? He surely did! God heard David and He forgave him. (Point to clean heart, #6c.)

Having been forgiven, David sang a glad song. (Have students turn to Psalm 32.) This is David's song: "Blessed (happy) is the person whose *TRANSGRESSION* is forgiven, whose *SIN* is covered. Blessed is the person whose *INIQUITY* the LORD does not count against him. I acknowledged my *SIN* to You, LORD God. I did not hide my *INIQUITY*. I said, 'I shall confess my *TRANSGRESSIONS* to the Lord.' And you forgave the *INIQUITY* of my *SIN*." As wicked as David had been, the LORD forgave his every sin! (See Psalm 32:1, 2, 5.)

JEHOVAH-Jireh provided a man (Nathan) who caused David to admit his wickedness.

JEHOVAH-Jireh provided prayer, so David could confess his sinfulness.

JEHOVAH-Jireh provided forgiveness when David turned back to Him.

JEHOVAH-Jireh will provide whatever you *need*.

3. JEHOVAH PROVIDES WHAT WE NEED
Psalm 23:1-3

What do you know about sheep? (*Teacher:* Encourage student discussion.) Sheep can be quite helpless. Yet they may be stubborn and want their own way. Left alone, they wander away. Or they may fall off a ledge and never get home. Sheep need a shepherd to care for them.

David was a shepherd when he was young. So he knew all about sheep. He wrote a psalm-song about a shepherd and his sheep. This song is in our Bible, Psalm 23. It is a part of the Bible which most people have memorized. Little children can quote it. Old people, dying, whisper it. It is a psalm which can help us every day and every night.

David's song begins, "The LORD (JEHOVAH) is my Shepherd" (Psalm 23:1). David is like every man, every woman, every boy, every girl. We all need someone to take care of us. Because David knew and loved the LORD, he could say, "The LORD (JEHOVAH) is my Shepherd." Are *you* a child of God? Have you been born into His family? If so, you, too, can say, "The LORD is my Shepherd." (*Teacher:* Have students repeat each section as you teach it.)

Show Illustration #7

Because the LORD was his Shepherd, David said, "I shall not want." Shepherds provide for their sheep. And JEHOVAH-Jireh provides for all who belong to Him. We should sing with David, "The LORD is my Shepherd, I shall not want." Never forget it; say it often; JEHOVAH-Jireh provides for everything I need.

David continued his song, singing, "He (the Lord [JEHOVAH]) makes me to lie down in green pastures" (Psalm 23:2a). Sheep must have green pastures. There they chew their food slightly, eating until they have had enough. Then they lie down and chew again what they had already swallowed. Sheep are perfectly content while they rest and chew their food in "green pastures."

Long after David lived, the Lord Jesus said, "I am the Bread of Life. He who comes to Me shall never hunger." And, . . . If anyone eats of this Bread, he shall live forever." (See John 6:35, 51.) Jesus was teaching that we need more than food to eat. We need to belong to Him, "the Bread of Life." When we are His, we have His eternal life and live forever.

The LORD my Shepherd "makes me lie down in green pastures." He also "leads me beside the still waters" (Psalm 23:2b). Sheep can't live without water. Yet they won't drink from a rushing torrent. So the shepherd provides quiet, still waters. We, too, must trust our Shepherd-Lord for drinking water.

But the Good Shepherd, our Lord Jesus Christ, taught that we need more than water to drink. We need "living water." And, said He, "Whoever drinks of the water that I shall give, shall never thirst. The water I shall give, will be a well of water springing up into everlasting life." (See John 4:10-14.) The person who receives the Lord Jesus as Saviour, receives His gift of everlasting life. As we need water for living on earth, so we need the Lord Jesus for life everlasting. JEHOVAH-Jireh provides food, water, and everlasting life.

"The LORD, my Shepherd," David added, "restores my soul" (Psalm 23:3a). I, the sheep, may be foolish. Wanting my own way, I may wander away from my Shepherd. (See Isaiah 53:6a.) But He searches for me, finds me, and brings me back. (See Luke 15:3-7.) He "restores" me if I have wandered from Him. When I sin, I must confess it to God and turn from it. And He will forgive me.

Because "the LORD is my Shepherd," he leads me in paths of righteousness for His name's sake" (Psalm 23:3). This means He leads me in right paths. He leads me in the way I should go. If I willfully wander to sinful places, my Shepherd LORD is not honored. And His name is dishonored. I must study His Word, so He can lead me to do right. (See Psalm 119:105.) JEHOVAH-Jireh provides His Word and His guidance.

4. JEHOVAH PROVIDES NOW AND FOREVERMORE
Psalm 23:4-6

Show Illustration #8

Sheep have enemies. There are lions, bears, snakes lurking about. But the Shepherd protects His sheep and lambs. "Even though I walk through the valley of the shadow of death, I shall fear no evil, for You [LORD] are with me. Your rod and Your staff comfort me" (Psalm 23:4). With His rod, the shepherd can kill wild animals. With His staff, He can rescue a sheep which falls over a cliff. So it is with me. Even if I am in the valley that may lead to death, I shall not be afraid. For my Shepherd-LORD, JEHOVAH-Jireh, will be with me in death's valley.

David also sang in his song: "You [LORD] prepare a table before me in the presence of my enemies. You anoint my head with oil; my cup overflows" (Psalm 23:5). Wild animals surround the sheep. But the shepherd cares for his sheep. He pours oil on the head of a wounded sheep. And he provides water for thirsty sheep. Just so, the LORD, my Shepherd, provides me with whatever I need.

The 23rd Psalm ends with this happy truth: "Surely goodness and mercy (*God's everlasting love*) shall follow me all the days of my life. And I shall live in the house of the LORD forever." (Psalm 23:6.) The house of the LORD is God's wonderful home in Heaven. JEHOVAH-Jireh provides a heavenly home for all who are His. (*Teacher:* Show JEHOVAH-Jireh poster.)

Are you truly a child of God? If so, you will have His goodness and tender love forever. Your Shepherd, JEHOVAH-Jireh, the LORD, provides everything you need. You may not always have all you *want*. Even then, His goodness and everlasting love will be yours. And some day you will be with Him in Heaven forever.

Long after David lived, God's Son, the Lord Jesus, came to earth. He said, "I am the Good Shepherd. The Good Shepherd gives His life for the sheep" (John 10:11). He, the Good Shepherd, provided Himself as the sacrifice for our sin. He died on the cross, taking our sins on Himself. (See 1 Peter 2:24.) But He did not stay dead. He arose from the grave. Soon He returned to Heaven where He is now as our Great Shepherd (see Hebrews 13:20-21). But some day He will come again. Then, He, the Chief Shepherd, will call all who are His. (See 1 Peter 5:4.) And we shall go up at once to be with Him forever.

Have you received God's Son, the Lord Jesus Christ, as your Saviour? If not, will you do so right now? He is the Good Shepherd and He will forgive your sin. Then you, too, will be able to say, "The LORD is *my* Shepherd." (*Teacher:* Enlarge on invitation as needed by your group.)

Lesson 3
JEHOVAH'S PEACE

Scripture to be studied: Psalm 40:6-10; 22:1-31; 16:10; 24:1-10

The *aim* of the lesson: To show that David prophesied of Christ.

What your students should *know*: Many of David's prophecies of Christ have already been fulfilled.

What your students should *feel*: Assured that every Bible prophecy will come true.

What your students should *do*: Study the Bible prophecies. Be certain of having God's peace in their hearts.

Lesson outline (for the teacher's and students' notebooks):

1. Prophecy of Christ's coming to earth (Psalm 40:6-10). (On earth, peace, Luke 2:14.)
2. Prophecies of Christ's death (Psalm 22:1-21). (Peace through the blood of His cross, Colossians 1:20.)
3. Prophecy of Christ's resurrection (Psalm 16:10). (The God of Peace raised Christ from the dead, Hebrews 13:20-21.)
4. Prophecy of Christ's coming as King (Psalm 2:1-10). (Peace in the Millennium, Revelation 20:4-6.)

The verse to be memorized:

The LORD will bless His people with peace. (Psalm 29:11b)

NOTE TO THE TEACHER

This is a lesson about PROPHECY. Prophecy often tells of correction for God's people in the present. Frequently PROPHECY tells ahead of time something which will happen later.

Many Bible prophecies have already been fulfilled. Others are yet to be accomplished. But in God's time, absolutely every Bible prophecy will come true. REMEMBER THIS: . . . All true prophecy closed with the completion of the Bible. God has not spoken through prophets since the book of Revelation.

Review the meanings of God's two names: (1) JEHOVAH *(the holy One who hates sin)*; (2) JEHOVAH-Jireh *(the LORD will provide)*. Another Hebrew name for God is JEHOVAH-Shalom. It means *The LORD our peace*. God the Father and God the Son are One. Therefore, what is true of God, is true of His Son, who said "Peace I leave with you, My peace I give unto you" (John 14:27). JEHOVAH-Shalom, *The LORD our peace*. So our study of PROPHECY includes the subject of PEACE.

On a poster print JEHOVAH-Shalom. On reverse side print, *The LORD our peace*.

Observe that Psalm 2 (point #4 of outline) does not indicate David wrote it. However, Acts 4:25 makes clear that David was the writer.

THE LESSON

What is the meaning of God's name, JEHOVAH? Did anything happen this week which reminded you of Him, the holy One who hates sin? (Encourage student response.) What did JEHOVAH-Jireh mean to you this week? Did He provide an answer to prayer?

Today we shall learn another wonderful name for the LORD God: JEHOVAH-Shalom. The first to use this name was Gideon. (He lived more than 100 years before the psalmist David.) Gideon and the people of God were in trouble. (See Judges 6:1-10.) So the LORD sent His angel to Gideon. Seeing God's angel terrified Gideon. (See Judges 6:11-22.) He was certain he was going to die. But the LORD told him, "Peace to you; do not be afraid. You will not die." (See Judges 6:23.)

Gideon was relieved, and happy, to know he would not die at once. So he built an altar to the LORD. He called it "JEHOVAH-Shalom, the LORD our Peace." (See Judges 6:24.) The LORD himself, JEHOVAH-Shalom, had given Gideon His peace. And He wants all His children always to have His peace. In one of David's psalms he wrote this wonderful promise: "The LORD will bless His people with peace" (Psalm 29:11). This is a verse you will want to memorize. (Have students read verse from their Bibles.)

Certain psalms David wrote were prophecies. He was telling ahead of time what would happen later. David would not have understood everything he wrote. (See 2 Peter 1:21.) But you and I can understand these prophecies. For some have already come true. And their fulfillment includes something about God's wonderful peace. Listen carefully!

1. PROPHECY OF CHRIST'S COMING TO EARTH (ON EARTH, PEACE)
Psalm 40:6-10; Luke 2:14

Once David wrote: "Here I am, I have come–it is written about Me in the Book [God's Law]. I love to do Your will, O My God." (See Psalm 40:7-8.) As he wrote, David would have wondered, *Of whom am I writing? God's Law Book tells nothing of me. And I do not always do God's will.* David could not understand what he wrote because he had written a prophecy from God.

Hundreds of years later this prophecy of David came true. The writer of the New Testament book of Hebrews explains, "When Christ came into the world, He said: '*Here I am, it is written about Me in the Book. I have come to do Your will, O God*'." (See Hebrews 10:5, 7.) David's prophecy was about Christ, written long, long before He was born.

Jesus Christ, God the Son, had always been with God the Father in Heaven. Before coming to earth, He offered to do God's will (Hebrews 10:7). So God prepared a body for Him.

Show Illustration #9

Christ was born on earth, a baby. He was laid in a manger. That night an angel announced His birth to shepherds. And a crowd of angels praised God saying, "Glory to God in the highest, and on earth peace among men in whom He is well pleased." (See Luke 2:8-14.)

Did you hear that? The angels declared, "On earth peace." JEHOVAH-Shalom, the LORD our peace, was on earth! He, the perfect One, came to do God's will. David, without understanding it, had prophesied this more than 1,000 years before!

2. PROPHECIES OF CHRIST'S DEATH (PEACE THROUGH THE BLOOD OF HIS CROSS)
Psalm 22:1-21; Colossians 1:20

David also wrote a very sad Psalm of prophecy. He began, "My God, My God, why have you forsaken Me?" (Psalm 22:1). He added, "All who see Me mock Me; they hurl insults, shaking their heads. They say, 'He trusts in the LORD; let the LORD rescue Him'" (Psalm 22:7-8). And "They pierced My hands and My feet. They divide My garments among them and cast lots for My clothing." (See Psalm 22:16, 18.)

Show Illustration #10

Long, long after David lived, the Lord Jesus was crucified on a cross. And He used the exact words of David's prophecy. He cried, "*My God, My God, why have You forsaken Me?*" (Matthew 27:46). The chief priests and leaders *mocked Jesus*. They sneered, "*He trusted in God; let God deliver him*" (Matthew 27:43). *The hands and feet of the Lord Jesus were pierced with nails.* (See John 20:25.) Why did God allow this? The gospel writer, John, tells the answer:

"That the Scripture might be fulfilled which says, 'They divided My garments among them, and cast lots for My clothing'" (John 29:23-24). What Scripture was fulfilled? The prophecy of David. (See Psalm 22:18.)

Years later the Apostle Paul wrote about Christ's death. He said Christ "made peace by the blood of His cross." (See Colossians 1:20.) Your sins separate you from God. But if you truly turn to Christ, claiming His provision for your sin, God forgives you. And He, JEHOVAH-Shalom, gives you His peace. It is yours because Christ shed His blood on the cross.

Was Christ's death the end? No, indeed!

3. PROPHECY OF CHRIST'S RESURRECTION (THE GOD OF PEACE RAISED CHRIST FROM THE DEAD)
Psalm 16:10; Hebrews 13:20-21

In another psalm, David prophesied again. He wrote, "You, God, will not let Your Holy One see decay" (Psalm 16:10). The bodies of all others would rot in their graves. But David prophesied that the Holy One would not decay in the grave!

Show Illustration #11

Hundreds of years later, the Apostle Peter preached: "God raised Jesus from the dead. It was impossible for death to keep its hold on Him. David prophesied about Him: '*You [God] will not let your Holy One see decay.*'" (See Acts 2:24, 27.) Another apostle, Paul, also quoted David's prophecy, saying: "*You [God] will not let your Holy One see decay.*" He added, "The One whom God raised from the dead did not see decay" (Acts 13:35-37). So the Holy One of whom David had prophesied, was Jesus, God's Son.

And David's prophecy came true! The Holy One, the Lord Jesus Christ, was raised from the dead.

Now listen to the words of this prayer: "May the God of peace (JEHOVAH-Shalom), who brought back from the dead our Lord Jesus, that Great Shepherd of the sheep . . . provide you with everything good to do His will" (See Hebrews 13:20-21.) JEHOVAH-Shalom raised Christ from the dead. And with that same amazing power, He will provide whatever you need to do His will.

We have learned all this today: (1) God's Holy Spirit caused David to prophesy that God's Son would come to earth. And He came. (2) The Spirit of God led David to prophesy that Christ would suffer and die. And He did suffer and die. (3) God's Spirit, through David, prophesied that the Lord Jesus would rise from the dead. And Christ arose.

David wrote yet other prophecies. In them he told that God's Son would reign on earth as King. (See Psalm 2:4-7.) This has not yet come true. But it will! For every Bible prophecy will be fulfilled in God's time.

4. PROPHECY OF CHRIST'S COMING AS KING (PEACE IN THE MILLENNIUM)
Psalm 2:1-7; Revelation 20:4-6

(*Teacher:* The many Scripture references in this section are for your personal study.)

Now hear this prophecy which David wrote! "The LORD says, 'I have set My King upon Zion, My holy hill'" (See Psalm 2:6.) The "King" is God's Son (Psalm 2:7). "Zion" is another name for the city of Jerusalem.

Show Illustration #12

So David's prophecy was this: A time is coming when God the Son will be King. And He will reign over all the earth for 1,000 years. (See Revelation 20:4-6.) This is called "The Millennium." The throne of God's Son will be in Jerusalem.

The Millennium will be a time of peace. Even wild animals will be tame. (See Isaiah 11:1-9.) The whole earth will be a safe place in which to live. (See Ezekiel 34:25-31.) There will be no war in the world. People will get along perfectly with each other. Why? The Lord Jesus Christ, the Prince of Peace, will reign on the earth. And JEHOVAH-Shalom is the LORD our peace. (See Psalm 24:3-10; 96:9-13; Isaiah 2:2-4; Micah 4:1-5. *Teacher:* Show JEHOVAH-Jireh poster.)

Near the end of the second psalm, David spoke to the rulers of earth. He warned: "Serve the LORD with fear." *Submit to God. Honor Him.* Then he closed, the psalm saying: 'Blessed [happy] are all who put their trust in the LORD [Christ, the Son].'" (See Acts 4:25-26.)

Have you placed your trust in God's Son? If so, He is your refuge from the punishment of sin. From the moment you became His, He lives within you forever. And He, JEHOVAH-Shalom, wants to fill your life with His peace. (*Teacher:* With meaning, read these verses to your students: John 14:27; 2 Thessalonians 3:16.) Remember God's promise: "The LORD will bless His people with peace" (Psalm 29:11).

If you have no peace, will you remain after class so we can talk together about this?

Lesson 4
PRAISE TO JEHOVAH

Scripture to be studied: Psalms 19, 146-150; 1 Chronicles 23:5; 2 Chronicles 5:12-14; Revelation 19:1, 3, 4, 6

The *aim* of the lesson: To show the importance of praising God.

What your students should *know*: The LORD God deserves praise.

What your students should *feel*: A desire to live a praise-filled life.

What your students should *do*: Determine to praise the LORD in everything always.

Lesson outline (for the teacher's and students' notebooks):

1. Creation praises God (the strong One) (Psalm 19:1-6).
2. God's Word praises JEHOVAH (the holy One) (Psalm 19:7-14).
3. Music-makers praise JEHOVAH (1 Chronicles 23:5; 2 Chronicles 5:12-14; Psalm 98:1, 3-6).
4. Heaven, earth, everyone will forever praise God (Psalms 146-150; Revelation 19:1, 3, 4, 6).

The verse to be memorized:

I will praise Thee, O LORD, with my whole heart; I will shew forth all Thy marvelous works. (Psalm 9:1)

> **NOTE TO THE TEACHER**
>
> The entire Bible, the Psalms particularly, challenge us to praise the Lord. Praise is telling the Lord we love Him. It is telling of His greatness. We praise Him for who He is and what he does. We praise him that He has all power (Psalm 21:13). We praise Him for his faithfulness (Psalm 89:5). We praise Him for His mighty acts (Psalm 145:4).
>
> The LORD deserves praise from everyone (Psalm 150:6). "God's way is perfect" (Psalm 18:30a). So we should praise Him for everything, good and bad, for "all things work together for good to those who love God" (Romans 8:28).
>
> Living a life of praise is very important for each Christian. Praise brings pleasure to God and blessing to you. May your life be a constant example of praise and thanksgiving.
>
> Prepare a poster to introduce God's name, ELOHIM.
>
> Print God (capital G: od in small letters) = ELOHIM.
>
> On reverse side print the meaning: The strong, faithful One.
>
> Use posters from previous lessons when you use the names of God or JEHOVAH.
>
> You may wish to introduce this lesson by reviewing Psalm 8 (see Lesson #1).
>
> We are grateful to Mrs. Charles Hufstetler (missionary who serves on our Editorial Board) for the excellent suggestion on praise which closes this lesson.

THE LESSON
1. CREATION PRAISES GOD
(The Strong One)
Psalm 19:1-6

When David was a shepherd, he watched his flock and studied the skies. Always he saw the darkness of night fade in the morning light. When David became king, he remembered what he had seen. So he wrote a wonderful song of praise, Psalm 19. In it, David uses the name *God* which, in his language, was *ELOHIM*. (Have students look at Psalm 19:1. Explain that *God* has a capital letter. The other letters are small. Display poster.)

When *God* is printed this way in the Bible, it refers to ELOHIM. And it means, "The strong, faithful One."

Show Illustration #13

David began his praise-song this way: "The heavens announce the glory of God (*Elohim, the strong, faithful One*). The skies show the work of His hands. Day and night they keep telling about God (*Elohim, the strong, faithful One*)." (See Psalm 19:1-2.)

Did the heavens and skies speak out loud to David? Can *you* hear them speak? No! David added this: "Without saying anything, the message of the heavens and skies goes to the whole world." (See Psalm 19:3.)

David's praise song continues: "The sun lives in the heavens where God–the *strong, faithful One*–placed it. The sun rises at one end of the heavens. It crosses to the other end. And nothing can hide from its heat." (See Psalm 19:6.)

David enjoyed seeing the skies, the stars, the moon, the sun. But he never, never worshiped them. He appreciated them because they reminded him of God–*Elohim, the strong, faithful One*. (See Psalm 19:1.) And God, he knew, was the One who created everything.

David loved God and His name, *Elohim*. He knew God is so strong that He simply spoke, and everything was created. He is so faithful that heavens and earth stay right where He placed them. David would have said over and over, "Elohim (God) is the strong One. He is the faithful One." No wonder David sang in his praise song, "The heavens announce the glory of God!"

We, too, are reminded of God's glory when we look at the heavens. We remember how wise and powerful God is to have created such wonders. But the heavens do not tell of His kindness. Nor do they explain God's great love for us. So in David's song, he tells another reason to praise God.

2. GOD'S WORD PRAISES JEHOVAH
(The Holy One)
Psalm 19:7-14

There were no Bibles like ours in the time of David. But many of God's words were on scrolls. To us, they would have looked like long rolls of paper. God's Law was written on those scrolls. (See Exodus 24:7.) The first five books of our Bible (Genesis, Exodus, Leviticus, Numbers, Deuteronomy) are God's Law.

When people worshiped God, they listened to His Law. The priest read God's Law from a scroll. From it, the people learned of the wonders of creation. They heard how Adam and Eve sinned against God. They understood that God chose the Jewish people for Himself. They realized how God cared for the Jews and gave them His laws, All this and much more was read from the scrolls.

Show Illustration #14

King David thought about the scrolls. So in his praise song, David told about God's Word written on those scrolls. And in the last part of Psalm 19 he did not sing of Elohim. Instead, he sang of the LORD (JEHOVAH–*the holy One who hates sin*). (Display poster.)

David sang: "The *law* of the LORD (*JEHOVAH*) is perfect" [as the LORD JEHOVAH is perfect]. (Psalm 19:7a.) The *law* told David what he should and should not do.

The *statutes* of the LORD (JEHOVAH) are to be trusted" (Psalm 19:7b), David sang. *Statutes* are God's truths. So David could trust the law of the LORD. For everything in His law is true.

"The *precepts* of the LORD (*JEHOVAH*) are right. They give joy to the heart" (Psalm 19:8a). *Precepts* are orders. When David obeyed JEHOVAH's orders, he was perfectly happy.

"The *commands* of the LORD (JEHOVAH) are pure" (Psalm 19:8b). David understood that God speaks with authority and He is always right.

David continued his song: "The *fear* of the LORD (JEHOVAH) is pure, lasting forever" (Psalm 19:9a). To *fear* JEHOVAH is to honor, reverence, and obey Him. Always David wanted to reverence and honor JEHOVAH, the holy One.

"The *judgments* of the LORD (JEHOVAH) are true and righteous altogether" (Psalm 19:9b). *Judgments* are decisions. God decides everything perfectly, never making a mistake. And He is never too severe with His punishment.

Of JEHOVAH's words David sang, "They are more precious than pure gold. They are sweeter than honey from the honeycomb. I am warned by Your words (JEHOVAH), and there is great reward in keeping and obeying them" (Psalm 19:10-11).

David enjoyed seeing God's glory in the heavens. But he was especially thankful that JEHOVAH, the holy One, provided His words on scrolls. From them he knew that JEHOVAH loved him and hated sin.

When David thought of the scrolls, he remembered JEHOVAH-Jireh, the LORD who provides. (Show poster.) God (*Elohim*) had provided His works (in the heavens) for David to see. The LORD (JEHOVAH) provided His words (on scrolls). And David praised the LORD GOD. Have *you* praised God for His creation and His Word? Have you praised Him that He, JEHOVAH-Jireh, provides everything you need?

David closed Psalm 19 with this prayer: (*Teacher:* read verses 13 and 14.) David asked the LORD to keep him from falling into sin. And he prayed that his words and thoughts would please the LORD. We all need to pray this same prayer.

3. MUSIC-MAKERS PRAISE JEHOVAH
1 Chronicles 23:5; 2 Chronicles 5:12-14; Psalm 98:1, 3-6

Young David had enjoyed praising God with his voice and his harp. When he was old, music was still important to him. So David chose 4,000 men to praise the LORD with musical instruments. (See 1 Chronicles 23:1-5.) Imagine that many in an orchestra!

David's son, Solomon, when he became king, built a magnificent temple for God. When it was finished, King Solomon called the people together to worship. There they offered more sacrifices than could be counted. (See 2 Chronicles 5:1-6.)

Show Illustration #15

After this great sacrifice to the LORD, there was marvelous music. All the Levites who were musicians were dressed in linen robes. They stood with 120 priests who played horns. The Bible says, "The trumpeters (horn-players) and singers joined as one. With their voices they praised the LORD, singing, 'God is good; His love lasts forever.' Then the temple of the LORD (JEHOVAH) was filled wirh a cloud. And the glory of the LORD filled the temple." (See 2 Chronicles 5:12-14.)

When you sing, do you remember you are singing to the LORD God of Heaven? If you play an instrument, do you use it to honor Him?

There are some people who cannot sing. Nor can they play an instrument. But they can speak their praise to God. Is it hard for you to express your praise to Him? Then read a Psalm which praises God. (For example, see Psalms 145, 146, 147.) As you read God's Word to Him, you will be singing silently. And He will hear your praise.

4. HEAVEN, EARTH, EVERYONE WILL FOREVER PRAISE GOD
Psalms 146-150; Revelation 19:3-7

The closing psalms prove the importance of praising God. Listen to part of Psalm 148. (*Teacher:* Use verses which are appropriate for your group.)

". . . Praise the LORD from the *heavens* . . . Praise Him, all His *angels* . . . Praise Him, *sun* and *moon*. Praise Him, all you *stars of light*. Praise the LORD from the *earth* and from the depths of the *ocean*. Praise the LORD . . . *fire, hail, snow, clouds*. Praise Him, you *stormy winds* . . . Praise Him, you *mountains* and *hills*. Praise Him, *fruit trees* and all *cedars*. You *wild animals* and all *cattle*, praise the LORD. Praise Him, *little creatures* and *flying birds*. Kings of the earth and *all nations*, praise the LORD . . . Praise Him all you *rulers on earth*, you *young people*, *old people* and *children* . . . Praise the LORD."

The last psalm commands all of us to praise the LORD: "Praise the LORD . . . for *His acts of power*. Praise Him for *His excellent greatness*. Let everything that has breath praise the LORD. Praise ye the LORD." You have breath, so this includes you. If you want to obey and please the LORD, praise Him!

Show Illustration #16

Some day everyone who has received the Lord Jesus as Saviour will be in Heaven. People from all over the world will be there. They will see the LORD on His throne and bow before Him. Then they will hear these words from the throne, "Praise our God, all you His servants, and you who fear Him, both small and great." (Revelation 19:5.)

Are you a child of God? If so, *you* will be in Heaven. And you will join with crowds (*multitudes*) exclaiming, "Hallelujah! For the Lord God all-powerful reigns!" (See Revelation 19:1-6.) You and all who belong to God will praise Him together. What a great day that will be!

Do you know how to praise the Lord here on earth? Do you know what to praise Him for? To start, let's go through the alphabet praising God for who He is and what He does. (*Teacher:* In English, start with the letter A.) Let students express their praise that God is able . . . God is above all . . . God is accessible. Praise Him that He is the burden bearer . . . a beacon . . . Praise Him that He cares . . . He comforts . . . He is the Creator. Students should make complete statements, giving praise for the exact ways He bore their burdens (for example), or cared for them.

Or students could use the letters in their names listing their praises to the Lord:

For example: Joan might praise the Lord this way:

Just–I praise you, Lord God, that You are just . . . You are always fair and You forgave me when I sinned and confessed it to You.

Omnipotent–I praise You that because You are omnipotent and have all-power, You protected me when I almost stepped in front of a car.

Accessible–I praise You that I can call on You at any time. When I cried to You in the middle of the night, You kept me safe when someone tried to break into our house.

Never-failing–I praise You that when I forgot what I was supposed to get at the store, you reminded me. And when I did not set my alarm clock, You woke me up in time.

Close with a time of thanksgiving and praise. Let one student thank Him that He is JEHOVAH, the holy One who hates our sin. Another can praise Him that He is JEHOVAH-Jireh, providing for absolutely every need, including our need of forgiveness. Someone else can praise Him that He is JEHOVAH-Shalom, the One who gives us peace, even in hard places. You, Teacher, can close with praise that He is ELOHIM, the faithful One who keeps us by His strength. Praise Him that we shall see Him in Heaven, and there praise Him face to face.

www.ingramcontent.com/pod-product-compliance
Lightning Source LLC
Chambersburg PA
CBHW060800090426
42736CB00002B/101